LifeCaps Presents:

Respect:

The Life and Times of Aretha Franklin

By Jennifer Warner

BookCaps™ Study Guides

www.bookcaps.com

Table of Contents

About LifeCaps

LifeCaps is an imprint of BookCaps™ Study Guides. With each book, a lesser known or sometimes forgotten life is recapped. We publish a wide array of topics (from baseball and music to literature and philosophy), so check our growing catalogue regularly (**www.bookcaps.com**) to see our newest books.

Introduction

Like most of the rivers flowing through the Mississippi Delta the Sunflower River is filled with mud from the bayous and small streams that feed it. That nutrient-rich silt also produces some of the best soil for growing cotton the earth has ever known. Following the Civil War so many freed slaves came to Sunflower County in western Mississippi to sharecrop that by 1900 more than three-quarters of the population of the county was African-American, including sharecropping families like those of Willie Walker and Rachel Pittman.

Willie and Rachel got married and three weeks into the year in 1915 they had a son they named Clarence LaVaughn. Willie left to serve in the Army when the United States got involved in World War I, and after he came back from Europe he abandoned the family for good. Clarence was barely four years old at the time. He often said the only thing his father ever taught him was how to salute.

Rachel quickly got married again to a man named Henry Franklin and the entire family adopted his surname. Clarence had a gift for speaking, and when he was just 16 years old he set out to become a preacher, traveling around the Mississippi Delta speaking to whatever congregation was willing to listen. He eventually became a regular preacher at the New Salem Baptist Church just across the Mississippi state line in Memphis, Tennessee. New Salem had organized only in 1928 in the home of Will and Sylvester Waddell, and the fellowship on Tillman Street was brimming with promise.

Clarence Franklin stayed at New Salem Baptist until 1943 when his calling took him out of the Deep South to Buffalo, New York to stand in front of the congregation at Friendship Missionary Baptist Church. The Friendship Church was exactly as old as Franklin, who became its fourth pastor in its 28 years. The Reverend Franklin stayed at Friendship only until 1946 but while there he helped launch a radio ministry broadcast on Sunday mornings.

The next stop for the Reverend C.L. Franklin, as he was now being called, would be his last. Franklin moved to Detroit, Michigan to start his own ministry which he christened the New Bethel Baptist Church. Franklin set up his new church in a hardscrabble section of Detroit known as Black Bottom. Although the mostly black neighborhood was known for its vibrant cultural milieu, its name derived not from its ethnic makeup but the dark, fertile topsoil the French had discovered when they first settled there in 1701. The same type of soil Clarence Franklin found under his fingernails growing up in the Mississippi Delta.

The Reverend Franklin would preside over New Bethel Baptist Church for the new three decades. He used the 4,500-seat sanctuary that he built on Hastings Street as a home base while he preached across the country. The fee to bring C.L. Franklin to town to deliver a sermon was a reported $4,000. When the reverend was seen driving around the streets of Detroit it was in a high-powered Cadillac. When he stepped out he would be sporting alligator skin shoes and sparkling diamond stickpins. Clarence Franklin was a celebrity.

C.L. Franklin was one of the first pastors to put his sermons on vinyl records. It was actually a Detroit record producer, Joe Von Battles, who did it first. After hearing Franklin's sermons on the radio, Von Battles recorded them over the air in his studio. Franklin eventually put dozens of sermons on wax for Battles' recording label, JVB Records. Some 50 Franklin sermons, usually preceded by a hymn, would later be licensed to legendary Chess Records. Sermons like "Dry Bones in the Valley" became famous and "The Eagle Stirreth Her Nest" would even be added to the National Recording Registry of the Library of Congress as one of the recordings that "are culturally, historically, or aesthetically important, and/or inform or reflect life in the United States."

One of the Reverend Franklin's admirers was a young pastor from Montgomery, Alabama named Martin Luther King, Jr. The two became fast friends and Franklin was drawn into the struggle for civil rights after King became involved in the Montgomery Bus Boycott in 1955. Back in Detroit he found similar causes right outside the New Bethel Baptist Church as he was able to help implement changes to end discrimination against black workers in the great automobile factories of Motor City.

The Reverend C.L. Franklin was not just famous for his stirring sermons. People also clamored to hear him sing. He even formed an a cappella group and picked up musical gigs in between speaking tours. Clarence Franklin came to be known as the man with the "Million Dollar Voice." If that moniker would be applied to his daughter decades later, that monetary denomination would be light by several orders of magnitude.

Chapter 1: Childhood

Clarence Franklin got married when he was eighteen years old but his union with Alene Gaines lasted scarcely a year. The reverend never spoke about his teenage marriage in future years, and history would never record how the two had met or where she lived or even how the marriage ended. But the experience matured him rapidly and he spent time in Greenville Industrial College that focused his ambitions on preaching as a serious career. And preaching to a devout congregation meant being married.

In 1935, Franklin's preaching duties found him in the small town of Shelby, Mississippi, as they often did. One day in church he met Barbara Vernice Siggers. Two years Clarence's junior and the middle child of seven children, Barbara's people had farmed in the Delta since the 1880s but she had been raised partly in the big city of Memphis. She was a reader and avid piano player. She also already had a son, giving birth to a little boy named Vaughn on Christmas Eve 1934. The biological father disavowed any relationship with Barbara or the boy.

Clarence married Barbara and adopted Vaughn; the little boy would almost reach adulthood before learning that the Reverend Franklin was not his real father. The couple quickly added a girl, Erma, and a boy, Cecil, of their own to the family. While Barbara helped Clarence out with his ministerial responsibilities the marriage was severely tested by the reverend's infidelities. The most damaging of his indiscretions took place in 1940 when Franklin had an affair with a 12-year girl from his Memphis New Salem Baptist congregation named Mildred Jennings in that resulted in the birth of an illegitimate daughter.

The marriage survived the scandal and Barbara continued to be a lively presence in the New Salem congregation, playing piano and singing with the choir. Mahalia Jackson, who was raised without parents in the barrios of New Orleans, and who went on to become the "Queen of Gospel," developed a close relationship with the Franklins and always maintained that Barbara was one of the country's great gospel singers and had even more natural talent as a singer than Clarence.

Barbara became pregnant again, and on March 25, 1942 another Franklin daughter was born in the small frame house at 406 Lucy Avenue in Memphis. Barbara and Clarence named her Aretha Louise. Two years later, Carolyn Ann joined the family and shortly after her birth the Franklins packed up their brood of five children and moved to Buffalo.

Marital discord, however, was not left behind in Tennessee. Women were drawn to the easy charm of Clarence Franklin and rumors began starting in Buffalo. After a short time in Detroit, Barbara wearied of Clarence's affairs, and she left the four children from their marriage in Michigan and returned to New York with Vaughn. The Franklins never divorced but they were never together again. Barbara would, however, make trips to Detroit and summers would find the children visiting their mother in Buffalo. Barbara found work in a music store and gave music lessons. She was attempting to rebuild her life as a nurse's aide when she died of a massive heart attack on March 7, 1952. She was only 34 years old.

With first the disappearance and then the death of her mother Aretha, not yet ten years old, was said to transform from a vibrant little girl to a more shy and insecure youngster. For a spell, Clarence's own mother, Rachel, came to Detroit to care for the children. They called her "Big Mama" and feared her discipline but Aretha also learned how to cook from her. Gospel singers, including Jackson and Frances Steadman and Marion Williams of the Famous Ward Singers, were frequent visitors to the Franklin house and a source of wonder and inspiration to Aretha.

Of all the stars who filtered in and out of the Franklin household young Aretha gravitated mostly to Clara Ward. Clara overcame a troubled childhood n Philadelphia, which included sexual abuse by a cousin, to shine in a family singing group founded by her oft-times overbearing mother, Gertrude. She recorded her first solo record in 1940 at the age of 16 and began touring nationally in 1943. The Ward Singers toured extensively, often on the bill with C.L. Franklin, and Clara's long-time romance with the reverend was said to bring her what little happiness she was able to derive from her overbearing family and fellow singers.

Since Clara Ward played the piano in addition to singing Aretha wanted to do both as well. She learned to play piano by ear and played for the congregation choir. She also sang and performed her first solo in church when she was twelve years old; in no time, Aretha was one of the three New Bethel Baptist featured soloists. At school she was often called on by the teachers to play piano and sing for the other students. When she wasn't playing music, her favorite pursuits were roller skating and watching boxing on the family's black and white television.

While Clara Ward and Mahalia Jackson made Aretha Franklin want to be a singer, James Cleveland taught her how to sing, stretching for notes she never imagined she could reach. James Edward Cleveland grew up in Chicago singing so much at Pilgrim Baptist Church that he eventually strained his vocal cords that ultimately gave him an immediately recognizable gravelly voice that he cultivated as he became one of the greatest gospel singers ever. Cleveland brought elements of traditional gospel, modern popular music and jazz into his arrangements to help create so-called modern gospel. Eventually he would win four Grammy Awards and a star on the Hollywood Walk of Fame. Cleveland taught Aretha not just how to sing notes and chords but how to put a song across to an audience.

Aretha picked up an entirely different education when she turned 14 and her father added her to his traveling gospel caravan. On the road she was thrust into a grown-up world where late nights and partying were the norm. She also learned about the realities of life in segregated 1950s America for blacks when the troupe was forced to find lodging and restaurants in out of the way establishments away from the mainstream white hotels and eateries.

During her first tour in 1956 Chess Records made arrangements to record C.L. Franklin's New Bethel Baptist Church gospel performances in the Oakland Arena in California. Later Chess would gather the performances together on an album called Songs of Faith. Still later, after Aretha Franklin soared to fame, this record was recognized for its value as an historical document. A raw Aretha's first appearance on record, accompanied only by a piano, would be re-released as The Gospel Sound of Aretha Franklin. Those used to the polished, powerful sounds of commercial Aretha Franklin records are likely taken back by shouts of "Amen!" and "Oh Lord!" that punctuate Songs of Faith.

Under her father's management, the teenage Aretha Franklin may have appeared to be groomed for a career in gospel. At the time, Detroit was teeming with young musical talent, most of whom would make their way to the Reverend C.L. Franklin's New Bethel Baptist Church at one time or another. Aretha was exposed to young singers like Otis Williams, Smokey Robinson and Diana Ross who would all go on to superstardom in the 1960s groups the Temptations, Miracles and Supremes, respectively. None would find fame pursuing gospel music.

But the performer who really started Aretha thinking that her future may lie elsewhere than gospel was Sam Cooke. Sam Cooke was a Chicago native who grew up singing gospel and performing in a religious group called the Soul Stirrers. He often made the drive to Detroit to sing at New Bethel Baptist and the Soul Stirrers appeared on the bill of Reverend Franklin's gospel caravan from time to time. Cooke had even made records such as "Touch the Hem of His Garment" and "Pilgrim of Sorrow."

Before returning home to Chicago, Cooke would often stop over the Franklin house and spend time with the family. Aretha developed an incurable crush on the slender Chicagoan with the smooth vocal style. She even created a scrapbook devoted entirely to him. Gradually Sam Cooke began to move musically beyond gospel. Then one day he came to Detroit not to sing at the New Bethel Baptist Church but to perform at a soul club in town, The Flame Show Bar.

After he signed with a new label called Keen Records Cooke stopped over the Franklins to play Aretha and her family a demo of his newest record that he was ready to release. It was "You Send Me." When the single was made public on September 7, 1957 it became a smash hit, reaching number one on both the Billboard rhythm and blues and pop charts. After that, 15-year old Aretha Franklin knew what she wanted from a singing career.

Aretha was not the only one who saw her future in popular music, not gospel. Two young songwriters who were regulars at the New Bethel Baptist Church were angling to get into record producing in the late 1950s. Berry Gordy, Jr. and Billy Davis got the break they were looking for when Jackie Wilson extricated himself from the singing quintet known as the Dominos and struck out on his own. Wilson went on to record seven straight hits written by Gordy and Davis who became the hottest duo in the music business.

They went looking for a female rhythm and blues singer who could record their songs and complement the success of Wilson. Their first choice was to sign the dynamic singer they heard in Reverend Franklin's church but the pastor would not allow his young daughter to sign a recording contract. Clarence Franklin was not opposed to the new style of music that was draining singing talent out of gospel - he was just convinced that Aretha was too young to expose to the music business.

The reverend did, however, allow Gordy and Davis to sign Aretha's older sister Erma. As it turned out, Aretha tagged along to the studio and played piano in rehearsals which meant she had to get paid musician scale and she became professional anyway. As it turned out, Erma preferred singing jazz and the Franklins were not recorded. The songs Gordy and Davis wrote for them became hits instead for Marv Johnson and Etta James. Aretha Franklin could have been the first female Motown star if the timing had been just a bit better.

But music was a strong pull from which Aretha would not be denied. Growing up in a motherless household with a celebrity father who was often away, Aretha was barely in her teens when she found herself pregnant. Her son Clarence was born on January 28, 1955, and less than two years later another boy, Edward, was born. Before she was fifteen years old, Aretha Franklin had two sons. She was forced to drop out of school but with the women of her extended family looking after the babies she never had to drop her plans for a music career.

Birth certificates for babies of married couples are a matter of public record in Michigan, but documents of illegitimate children are sealed and available only to the birth mothers. Aretha Franklin never chose to speak publicly about her first two sons, and any information as to the fathers or the circumstances around which the children were brought into the world are unknown. The only light being a teenage mother shed on Aretha Franklin's life was establishing a foundation for a troubled adulthood marked with victimization by men.

Chapter 2: Rise to Fame - Columbia Years

When she turned 18 years old Clarence Franklin was ready to give his consent to his daughter signing a recording contract. Sam Cooke counseled her to go with RCA, the label that he recorded for, and under normal circumstances that endorsement from her dream singer would have made her joining the RCA stable a certainty. But that would be in a world without John Hammond.

Hammond was born in New York City on December 15, 1910, descended from the richest man of the 19th century, Commodore Cornelius Vanderbilt. When he showed a passion for music at an early age young John was steered into a training program of classical music. But when he reached his teens he began forsaking the New York concert halls for the jazz clubs of uptown Manhattan where black musicians were fueling the Harlem Renaissance of the 1920s and 1930s.

Hammond dutifully enrolled at Yale University to study violin but he dropped out after two years to plunge himself into the emerging popular music industry. He landed a job as the first American correspondent for the English music magazine *Melody Maker*, and when he was twenty years old, Hammond bankrolled a record by pianist Garland Wilson that became a minor hit. Soon the young heir was living among the Bohemians in Greenwich Village and working to bring black music into the American mainstream.

He invested in The Café Society, America's first integrated nightclub and appealed relentlessly to Benny Goodman, the country's most popular bandleader, to work with black musicians for the first time. As a talent scout for Columbia Records he produced Bessie Smith, Count Basie, Billie Holiday, Big Joe Turner and others to the label. He was ready to break Robert Johnson before the legendary bluesman died under shadowy circumstances in 1938 at the age of 27.

After his career was sidetracked by World War II and the collapse of his family's fortune, Hammond rejuvenated the American folk music landscape by signing Pete Seeger and then Bob Dylan to Columbia contracts. Dylan and his eclectic voice had impressed no record executives as he made the rounds of New York's folk clubs. When Hammond heard him he signed the Minnesota troubadour immediately, which caused others in the industry to sneer that it was "Hammond's Folly."

Hammond first heard Aretha Franklin sing on a demo tape that was one of four delivered to his office by composer Curtis Lewis. As her teenage years passed, Aretha had become more and more enthralled by the blues singing of Dinah Washington. The two had much in common. Washington was born in the Deep South, in Tuscaloosa, Alabama. She sang gospel music in her teens after moving to Chicago and won several talent contests. When she reached her twenties she transitioned into blues singing and became the premier black female recording artist of the 1950s. All the while Washington retained a vocal style that could move smoothly through all genres of music. All of this made a young Aretha Franklin determined to have a career like Dinah Washington's. Unfortunately her off-stage life would come to mirror the flamboyant Washington's as well; Dinah had seven husbands before dying of a drug overdose at the age of 39.

After Clarence Franklin conceded that Aretha's future in music lay in popular music and not gospel she packed her bags and left Detroit for New York City. She checked in to the YWCA on East 38th Street before moving in with her manager Jo King. Major "Mule" Holley, a jazz bassist who had accompanied Charlie Parker and Ella Fitzgerald and who was a friend of Clarence Franklin, arranged to take the 18-year old Aretha into a recording studio to produce a demo of a blues song, "Today I Sing the Blues."

Hammond was not impressed by the four songs that Lewis had brought to him. But the woman playing piano and singing on "Today I Sing the Blues" made an excited impression. Hammond would later recall in his memoirs that it was the best voice he had heard since encountering a 17-year old Billie Holiday for the first time in Monette Moore's Club on 133rd Street in Harlem a quarter-century earlier.

When King learned of Hammond's interest in Aretha she invited him over to meet the Detroit newcomer in a small recording studio she operated at 1697 Broadway. Hammond was immediately convinced he was hearing the future of the blues. Aretha Franklin would sign her first recording contract with Hammond and Columbia Records, a six-year deal that produced ten original albums and a pair of packaged "greatest hits" collections.

John Hammond was the first producer to take his new discovery into the recording studio, teaming her with Ray Bryant's jazz combo. Raphael Homer Bryant was another precocious musical talent, turning professional while still in his Philadelphia high school in the 1940s. When Hammond had returned to Columbia Records in 1959, the jazz pianist had been his first signing. To make sure his two prized clients got along, Hammond brought Bryant and Franklin together for an impromptu performance at the celebrated Village Vanguard jazz club in Greenwich Village. The duo clicked immediately and Aretha moved into her first recording session along with the Ray Bryant Combo on August 1, 1960.

Four songs were recorded in that historic session. Three - "Today I Sing the Blues," "Right Now," and "Love Is the Only Thing" - were selected by Hammond. The fourth, Judy Garland's calling card, "Over the Rainbow," was added at Aretha's insistence. It established a pattern of participation in song selection on her albums that Franklin would maintain throughout her career. The quartet became the backbone for Aretha Franklin's debut album, Aretha: With The Ray Bryant Combo. Ahead of the album's release "Today I Sing the Blues" became the first single and eventually climbed to #10 on the United States rhythm and blues charts for the unknown teenager.

Frank Driggs, a Columbia record producer who worked with Hammond and who would amass what was roundly agreed to be the world's finest collection of jazz photographs, provided the breathless liner notes on Aretha: With The Ray Bryant Combo: "The word is out. A magnetic new artist, Aretha Franklin, only a short while away from her father's gospel church in Detroit, has been breaking up audience in theatres and nightclubs throughout the country and on Columbia single records. Combining a completely natural and uninhibited vocal style with an irresistible rhythmic sense, Aretha Franklin has established herself as one of the hottest new performers in show business and one likely to set new standards in the entertainment industry. She doesn't just open the door - she breaks it down."

While the music men at Columbia Records were certain they had uncovered the next great star, the business executives struggled with how to market Aretha to the music world. Her debut album was a cornucopia of jazz, blues and pop songs with a few standards tossed into the mix. It proved a talisman for Aretha's career at Columbia. Over the course of six years her first song to chart on the Billboard Hot 100 was "Won't Be Long," a jazz song. But her first Top 40 single came from "Rock-a-Bye Your Baby with a Dixie Melody," a standard that had debuted on Broadway in 1918 during a production of the musical Sinbad. While several Franklin tunes cracked the rhythm and blues charts she also had "Easy Listening" success with ballads. At the same time Columbia was booking its "new star female vocalist" on television rock-and-roll shows such as the teenage dance show American Bandstand, the ABC musical variety series Shindig! and Hollywood A Go-Go, a Los Angeles based party show frequented by the likes of Lesley Gore, Sonny & Cher and Smokey Robinson & the Miracles. There was no musical genre that was definitively Aretha Franklin.

Political machinations behind the scenes did Aretha's recording career no favors either. John Hammond was removed after their second album together, ending any chance for his vision of Franklin as the touchstone for blues singers. In 1961, Aretha jettisoned Jo King as her manager in favor of Ted White, a man she was introduced to in a Detroit club called The 20 Grand by singer Della Reese. Six months later she was Mrs. Ted White and, despite having no prior experience, White was soon managing his new bride.

White saw Aretha as the next jazz star, following in the footsteps of Billie Holiday and Dinah Washington. He bristled at attempts by Columbia to channel her talents elsewhere making life unpleasant for Aretha around her record company. Home life was not much different as White reacted angrily whenever Aretha expressed interest in different styles of music. He also developed a contentious relationship with Reverend Clarence Franklin, essentially placing himself on the opposite side of everything that mattered to his wife.

For her part Aretha reacted more or less passively to being buffeted about by those pulling her one way or another musically. She had confidence that she would one day be successful and was comforted by the realization that her Columbia contract was not forever. She gave birth to a third child, Ted White, Jr., in 1964 but the marriage was continually confrontational and frequently violent. After the inevitable divorce in 1969 Aretha was to speak to Ted only two more times and never spoke about her first husband publicly.

Over the course of six years, Columbia never seemed to grasp exactly what it had in Aretha Franklin. Much of the material from her ten albums with the label would eventually be reissued after she achieved superstardom and those tracks are now considered essential recordings of the young artist. But nothing was to come of the records in their time. After her contract expired, the one-time "future of the blues" slipped quietly away from Columbia Records.

Chapter 3: Commercial Success - Atlantic Years

Like Aretha Franklin, Rick Hall's people were Mississippi sharecroppers. By his teens, he too had escaped the fields and was preparing for a job as a tool and die man in Rockford, Illinois while playing in local bar bands. He returned to the South after the Korean War as a family man, but after his father and wife both died within weeks of one another he decided to devote himself to music. By the late 1950s Hall and his partner, saxophonist Billy Sherrill, were writing hit songs for the likes of Brenda Lee and Roy Orbison that helped provide seed money for a recording studio Hall built in Muscle Shoals, Alabama, a small town of some 4,000 people situated on a hard bend in the Tennessee River.

Hall put together a studio band and began to produce hit records for artists who were increasingly finding their way to Muscle Shoals from New York and Los Angeles and even London. He built a reputation as a white Southern producer who could make hit records with black Southern soul singers. By the time he made Percy Sledge an international star with the searing "When a Man Loves a Woman," Hall had improbably turned the remote outpost of Muscle Shoals into a mecca in the music world.

Music producers everywhere were interested in getting a dose of that "Muscle Shoals sound." One of Hall's biggest boosters was Jerry Wexler of Atlantic Records. Wexler had been a writer for Billboard magazine when he was recruited to Atlantic in 1953. Ray Charles was the label's biggest star at the time and Wexler began calling his brand of music "rhythm & blues" which came to replace the long-used industry term "race music" for the recordings of black musicians. After Hall opened his FAME (Florence Alabama Music Enterprises) Recording Studios Wexler started shipping his acts to the industrial looking building on West Avalon Street in Muscle Shoals to cut records.

Working his magic behind the board Hall engineered hits for Wilson Picket, Otis Redding and James and Bobby Purify. Wexler also thought his newest act, Aretha Franklin, could benefit from a trip to Muscle Shoals. Wexler had first heard Aretha sing on the records she made for Chess when she was fourteen years old. He had followed her career at Columbia and thought she was making great records but was as perplexed as anyone else in the industry over the constant shifting of her sound. He bided his time and when Franklin's contract with Columbia expired then signed her for Atlantic Records. Then Wexler sent Aretha to FAME and Rick Hall with a mandate to sing the blues.

She set out for Alabama with her husband, engineer Tom Dowd and a song penned by Ronnie Shannon. Backed by the Muscle Shoals Rhythm Section and playing piano, Aretha tore into a version of "I Never Loved a Man (The Way I Love You)" that electrified everyone in the studio. When it was released on January 4, 1967 the single roared up the Billboard Hot 100 pop charts and peaked at number nine. On the Rhythm and Blues charts it rode all the way to number one. Aretha Franklin had her first hit song and the first defining song of her career.

A B-side called "Do Right Woman, Do Right Man" was in the works as well when White fired trumpeter Melvin Lastie from the session after he thought the horn player was flirting with Aretha. Hall went to the Whites' motel room that night to make amends but wound up in a fist fight instead. The session was canceled and the Atlantic Records entourage returned to New York. Wexler broke off relations with Hall but recruited the Muscle Shoals Rhythm Section, known familiarly as The Swampers, to come to New York and finish the record. Jerry Wexler had unlocked the secret to making the 25-year old Aretha Franklin a superstar.

On March 10, 1967 Aretha's first full album for Atlantic Records was released, also named "I Never Loved a Man the Way I Love You". The record was quickly certified gold and rumbled all the way to number two on the Billboard album chart. Thirty-five years later the album had lost none of its power to thrill and *Rolling Stone* magazine listed it as the number one record on its "Women in Rock: 50 Essential Albums" list.

Garnering even more recognition was the lead song on the album. Wexler brought Aretha a song originally written as a ballad two years earlier by Otis Redding. Redding had recorded the tune for his Stax label in an uptempo style but Aretha took "Respect" to an entire new energy level. Aretha's sisters Erma and Carolyn sang back-up and the Franklin girls worked out its signature "Sock it to me, Sock it to me, Sock it to me, Sock it to me…" chorus line. Carolyn came out with the idea to spell out the now iconic "R-E-S-P-E-C-T."

"Respect" became Aretha's first number one hit on the Billboard Hot 100. When 1968 awards season rolled around she won the first two Grammys of her career for "Best Rhythm & Blues Recording" and "Best Rhythm & Blues Solo Vocal Performance, Female." Twenty years later the song would be inducted into the Grammy Hall of Fame and Rolling Stone slots it as the number five song on its "500 Greatest Songs of All Time."

Her new fame crystallized on February 16, 1968 when she performed at a sold-out Cobo Arena in Detroit for what had been declared "Aretha Franklin Day." She received plaques acknowledging her sweep of the music industry awards as "Female Vocalist of the Year" and Martin Luther King, Jr. flew in for the 90-minute concert and to present her with the Southern Christian Leadership Council Drum Beat Award for Musicians.

But just two months later on April 9 Aretha was called upon to sing "Precious Lord, Take My Hand" at the funeral of Dr. King, her father's friend who she had known since childhood. The gospel hymn penned by the Reverend Thomas A. Dorsey in 1932 was Dr. King's favorite song and he had instructed associates to play the hymn at the mass he was planning to attend in Memphis on the night he was shot on his motel balcony. The Reverend King often brought Mahalia Jackson on stage to sing the hymn at civil rights rallies. Four years later Aretha Franklin would sing another heart-rending rendition of "Precious Lord, Take My Hand" at Mahalia Jackson's funeral.

Wexler would continue to guide Aretha's career at Atlantic Records for the next nine years until he left for Warner Brothers in 1975. The two would team to create twelve albums, four of which were certified gold and six that topped the rhythm and blues charts. He would later describe what he accomplished with Aretha simply as, "I took her to church, sat her down, and let her be herself."

That self was also transforming along with her music. During her Columbia days, Aretha Franklin was content to present a conservative persona, one that traveled demurely along with the material she was asked to record. With Atlantic, her raw, earthy voice was more out front of the songs, and she, too, emerged with a flashier style, favoring slinky dresses slathered in sequins. In the 1970s when the Black Power Movement emerged from the Civil Rights Movement she adopted Afro-centric clothing and her bouffant hairdos relaxed into a more natural Afro hairstyle.

Wexler also attributed Aretha's breakthrough at Atlantic Records to her musicianship, "In my opinion, one of the reasons that we clicked right away was because I put Aretha at the piano. When a musician who writes can play anything, I like to have them play on that record - whether he can play or not. It happens that Aretha is a magnificent player. At Columbia they didn't avail themselves - or only occasionally - of having her be part of the rhythm section. But by having the soloist, or the featured artist who's going to be singing on the record, by having him put his input into the track, it puts you in a whole different level of game."

Wexler and Franklin clicked from the beginning with two gold albums and six Top Ten singles in their first year of collaboration. Aretha covered material from the Rolling Stones, Frank Sinatra, Lennon and McCartney and Willie Nelson as she built her reputation as the Queen of Soul through the 1960s. She had a way of slanting almost any material to make it distinctively hers. When a song by Don Covay about field hands working in the Deep South was brought to her Aretha transformed "Chain of Fools" into an anthem about a string of hapless lovers. It became another defining hit single.

As Aretha morphed into an international star the jagged edges of her personal life were laid bare. And there always seemed to be something for an eager press to write about. The troubles in her marriage were an open secret; Ted had struck her once in public and had plugged her new production manager with a bullet. Clarence Franklin was indicted by the government on charges of evading income taxes and forced to pay a $25,000 fine. He was also arrested for marijuana possession. Aretha had run afoul of the law as well - she was arrested for reckless driving in 1968 and hauled in for disorderly conduct the next year as she was rumored to be drinking heavily. A cover story in *Time* magazine in 1968, which many other artists would see as a career-building triumph, was so negative about her turbulent private life that the ever-shy and insecure Aretha stopped giving interviews to the press for years.

The one place she grew more confident during the Atlantic years was on stage. With a string of actual hits that audiences wanted to hear Aretha became more sure-footed in performing them. She shed the stage fright that dogged her early concerts and used her time on stage as an escape from her personal demons. Free of her marriage to Ted White in 1969 the new decade of the 1970s continued to find Aretha's personal life in disarray. An affair with her new road manager produced her fourth son in 1970. The little boy was named Kecalf, a jumble of letters pulled from the names of his parents: Aretha Louise Franklin and Kenneth E. Cunningham. Franklin and Cunningham would remain together for six years but never made it to the altar.

Nothing could stop the Aretha Franklin hit machine in the early 1970s, however. Between 1970 and 1972 she charted with 11 singles, five of which became gold records and four that rose to number one on the rhythm and blues charts. "Don't Play That Song (You Lied)" was a cover of a tune released a decade earlier by soul singer Ben E. King, one-time lead singer of the Drifters. King's wife Betty Nelson had written the song which went to number two on the Rhythm and Blues singles charts for King; Aretha's plaintive version with the Dixie Flyers ruled the same charts for five weeks.

Franklin also recorded another of King's popular hits, "Spanish Harlem," which was written by Jerry Leiber and Phil Spector. "Spanish Harlem" has been covered by many artists in many genres but no one took it to the heights that Aretha did in 1971. New Orleans musical chameleon Dr. John played keyboards, funkmaster Bernard "Pretty Purdie" was on drums and Chuck Rainey, a favorite session player, handled the bass. "Spanish Harlem" rose to number two on the Billboard pop charts while becoming one of Aretha's biggest selling records overseas.

Aretha put her spin on another popular song when she recorded a gospel-tinged rendition of Simon & Garfunkel's "Bridge Over Troubled Water" and drove it to the top of the rhythm and blues charts just months after the original had sold six million copies. Aretha's performance would win her a Grammy Award for "Best Female R&B Performance." This was hardly news in 1972 at the National Academy of Recording Arts and Sciences - she won the Grammy Award for vocal performance every year between 1968 and 1975, so many times that the R&B category was often slyly referred to as "The Aretha Award." Along the way she was collecting more million-selling records at Atlantic than any woman in recording history.

Jerry Wexler worked hard to insure that his biggest act would not be trapped in the niche of soul singer, no matter how profitable that was proving to be. He was determined to bring Aretha's voice to the widest possible audience. To that end Wexler arranged for Aretha to perform at Fillmore West in San Francisco managed by Bill Graham, the most famous rock and roll concert hall there ever was.

Wulf Wolodia Grajonca was born in Berlin, Germany in 1931 and grew up in an orphanage. A fortunate pre-Holocaust exchange of Jewish orphans for French Christian orphans got Wulf out of Nazi Germany in 1941, and even more fortunately, he was part of a small coterie of children who escaped all the way to the shores of the United States. After working hard to master English he pulled the name "Graham" out of the phone book before serving in the Korean War. In the early 1960s Graham made his way to the Bay Area where he hooked up with a radical theater group called the San Francisco Mime Troupe. After organizing a benefit concert for the Mime Troupe he decided to go into the promoting business full-time.

Graham's Fillmore Auditorium at 1805 Geary Street became the nexus for the counterculture music scene of the late 1960s. The Fillmore was practically the home stage for such acts as the Jefferson Airplane, Santana, Jimi Hendrix, Frank Zappa, Creedence Clearwater Revival and many more. Between 1965 and 1969 the Grateful Dead took the stage at the Fillmore Auditorium 51 times.

On March 5, 1971, Aretha Franklin became the first rhythm and blues singer to play at the Fillmore. Wexler had to make concessions to make the historic night happen. He promised a skeptical Graham that once "these longhairs" hear Aretha sing they would embrace her like Sly and the Family Stone, Janis Joplin or any of the acts that were typical Fillmore fare. Unlike the Vegas casinos and concert halls Franklin had been used to playing, the smaller Fillmore had no chairs and the audience sat cross-legged on the floor or, when the spirit moved them, got up to groove to the sounds. Wexler had to pledge that Atlantic would pick up the shortfall in revenue from the Fillmore which he planned to cover by releasing a live album of the performance.

Aretha opened her concert with a nuclear-powered rendition of "Respect" and from the opening chords it was evident that Graham need not worry how the laid-back Fillmore crowd would respond to the Queen of Soul. Even so Wexler had made sure to include Aretha's interpretation of many of the famous "hippie anthems" that were normally heard at the Fillmore. On the set list she covered Stephen Stills' "Love the One You're With" and the Beatles' "Eleanor Rigby" and "Make It with You" from David Gates and Bread. Backing her was saxophone virtuoso King Curtis and his band the Kingpins.

Aretha's engagement at the Fillmore was three nights and by Sunday evening her appearance before a crossover audience was a complete triumph. But the Queen of Soul managed to top even herself with the final act on Sunday. For her encore she walked back on stage with Ray Charles dangling from her arm. The two performed a nearly nine-minute spontaneous version of "Spirit in the Dark" for an enraptured audience. It was a highlight of Wexler's long career in music to bring his two singing idols together and he lamented that he was never able to get Franklin and Charles to cut a complete album together.

Aretha Live at Fillmore West was released on May 19, 1971 with ten tracks. It became a top ten album on the Billboard charts and a number one best selling record on the rhythm and blues charts as it was certified gold. The only sad note surrounding the Fillmore appearance happened that summer when King Curtis was stabbed and killed in an altercation with drug dealers outside his apartment in New York City. In 2005, five years after he was inducted into the Rock and Roll Hall of Fame, Rhino Records released a definitive four-CD box set of the three nights at the Fillmore called Don't Fight The Feeling: The Complete Aretha Franklin & King Curtis Live At Fillmore West.

Back in the studio, Wexler guided Aretha through Young, Gifted and Black which became her most highly regarded album of the 1970s. Aretha interpreted material from the finest contemporary songwriting teams of the day including John Lennon and Paul McCartney, Bernie Taupin and Elton John, and Burt Bacharach and Hal David. But the songs that provided the album's greatest emotional impact were ones written by Franklin herself, "Rock Steady" and "Day Dreaming." It was the dawning of the age of the singer-songwriter and Aretha Franklin's efforts could stand alongside those of Carole King and Carly Simon and Joni Mitchell. Young Gifted and Black, which took its title from a Nina Simone song, produced five hit singles, was certified gold and won Aretha yet another Grammy Award.

The album was the musical expression of Aretha's relationship to the culture of the early 1970s, as she explained to the music press. "I believe that the black revolution certainly forced me and the majority of black people to begin taking a second look at ourselves. It wasn't that we were all that ashamed of ourselves, we merely started appreciating our natural selves…sort of, you know, falling in love with ourselves just as we are. We found that we had far more to be proud of. So I suppose the revolution influenced me a great deal, but I must say that mine was a very personal evolution - an evolution of the me in myself."

A year later Wexler arranged another live album for Aretha, this time recording a gospel set at the New Temple Missionary Baptist Church in Los Angeles. The Reverend James Cleveland, who had pushed a teenage Aretha to go after notes she didn't believe she could reach, was at the piano and conducting the Southern California Community Choir. Her father, the Reverend C.L. Franklin officiated at the service. Amazing Grace was released on June 1, 1972 as a double album and became the biggest selling gospel album of all time. After sales passed two million units Amazing Grace was certified double platinum and remains the biggest selling record in Aretha Franklin's career that spans over a half-century. The only disappointment with the project was that a documentary film about the performance directed by Sydney Pollack, coming off an Oscar nomination for *They Shoot Horses, Don't They?*, was shelved by Warner Brothers and never released.

As the 1970s trundled on Aretha's relationship with Ken Cunningham evolved into one of the happiest of her life. Unlike Ted White, Cunningham was content to remain in the shadows of Aretha's career, even as she relied greatly on his opinions. The good times with Cunningham helped Franklin cut back on her drinking and he encouraged her in her constant battles to lose weight. Early in their relationship Aretha would appear on album covers shrouded in African scarves and loose-fitting clothing. By 1975 she had dropped 40 pounds and the 125-pound Aretha would be clothed on album covers covered only by a strategically placed white fur.

For years, Aretha Franklin could always find comfort in her phenomenal commercial success to assuage the disappointments of her personal life. But in the mid-1970s as she enjoyed some of the first tranquil domestic years of her adulthood her magic at selling records suddenly dried up. In 1974 Aretha put out Let Me in Your Life which, like seven of her previous albums with Atlantic Records climbed into the number one spot on the rhythm and blues charts (the other four made it to number two). Let Me in Your Life produced three hit singles but overall critical reception was lukewarm.

Neither of her next two studio efforts, With Everything I Feel in Me and You, cracked the Top 40 albums on the Billboard Hot 100 charts, the first time that had happened since Aretha signed with Atlantic Records a decade earlier. Excuses and explanations began careening around the music industry. The song selection was weak. Musical tastes were shifting. Disco was all the public wanted to buy. The records were overproduced with synthesizers that overwhelmed even Aretha's voice. Maybe it was because Jerry Wexler was already mentally out the door at Atlantic Records. By the time Wexler left officially in 1975 the word "comeback" was being whispered in connection with Aretha's name.

Aretha's record selling slump coincided with the arrival of a new female rhythm and blues star who was being called "the new Aretha Franklin" even though the original Aretha Franklin had barely passed her 30th birthday. Natalie Cole was the daughter of the treasured 1950s singer Nat King Cole. The energetic Natalie not only ended Aretha's eight-year stranglehold on Grammy awards but between 1975 and 1979 she piled up six consecutive gold albums. During that same period Aretha Franklin scored only one gold record and that was a soundtrack album to the 1976 Warner Brothers film Sparkle about a girl group trying to crack the big time in 1950s Harlem.

Rolling Stone magazine looked over the rhythm and blues landscape and concluded, "Reviewers have pointed to Cole's reliance on numerous Franklin trademarks. The comparisons are all the more dramatic because Aretha is characterized in the media as an aging Queen of Soul, in decline. Aretha has not responded well to it. At Atlantic Records, it is said, she was jealous of Roberta Flack's success and the attention she was getting from Atlantic executives. Aretha's morale was kept up only by such token honors as Grammy Awards. And then last year along came Natalie Cole."

"Aging" Queen of Soul she may well have been but Aretha, a lifelong Democrat, was invited to sing at President Jimmy Carter's inauguration, in January 1977. While fellow invitee Linda Ronstadt performed a Willie Nelson tune, "Crazy," Aretha plowed patriotic ground at the John F. Kennedy Center for the Performing Arts with a version of Irving Berlin's "God Bless America." Keeping with Jimmy Carter's southern roots Duane Allman handled the rock and roll at the Inaugural Ball.

At the same time Aretha was fumbling for direction in the musical wilderness her relationship with Ken Cunningham was disintegrating. Early in 1977 at a benefit in Los Angeles organized by football star-turned actor Roosevelt Grier, Aretha was introduced to a New York City-born actor named Glynn Turman. Like Aretha, Turman got started in show business early, appearing at the age of 13 on Broadway with Sidney Poitier and Ruby Dee in *Raisin in the Sun*. He broke into the movies in blaxploitation films of the early 1970s and had recently had the lead as Leroy "Preach" Jackson in the cult hit Cooley High.

The two started dating and the press sizzled with the fact that Aretha was four years older than her new paramour, casting her as an "older woman," an unwelcome spotlight on her age at the same time the music press was preparing her obituary. Nonetheless, when Turman, who had been married before and had kids, proposed marriage later in the year Aretha excitedly accepted and the couple was married in Detroit on April 11, 1978. Clarence Franklin performed the ceremony at New Bethel Baptist Church and Stevie Wonder sang "Isn't She Lovely" as the bride-to-be made her way to the altar.

Aretha's wedding to Glynn would be one of the last happy days she would spend with her father. On June 10, 1979 while Aretha was performing at the Aladdin Hotel and Casino in Las Vegas the Reverend was in his Detroit home watching television when burglars broke into the two-story brick house, expecting it to be unoccupied. Franklin was shot twice in the groin and once in the knee. The pastor was rushed to Henry Ford Hospital for emergency surgery to repair a ruptured artery. He recovered briefly before slipping into a coma from which he never woke up, lingering for five years before dying in 1984 at the age of 69.

A rare highlight as the 1970s drudged to a close saw Franklin recognized with a star on the Hollywood Walk of Fame, installed on the south side of the 6900 block of Hollywood Boulevard. In 1979 Aretha decided to end her relationship with Atlantic Records which had been one of the most lucrative in recording history. Since the release of the soundtrack album Sparkle in 1976 her three follow-up albums had cratered and Aretha was feeling neglected by the label. It was time to find a new musical home.

Chapter 4: Comeback - Arista Years

Clive Davis grew up on the streets of Brooklyn cheering for the Dodgers in baseball's National League and winning awards for scholarship in school. Mostly out of obligation Davis went through New York University Law School and pursued a job with a top law firm in New York City. Far from smitten by the law Davis was thrilled when he was assigned as counsel to one of the firm's clients, Columbia Records. Davis started working with Columbia about the same time a young Aretha Franklin was making her first records in a different part of the building.

In 1967, the year Aretha departed, Davis got his chance to run Columbia Records. Showing that he had a knack for more than just contracts, one of his first signings to the label was Janis Joplin. Acts like Laura Nyro, Simon & Garfunkel, Chicago, Billy Joel and Bruce Springsteen followed and Davis transformed Columbia from a stodgy, muddled label - the type that could not figure out how to use an Aretha Franklin - into the hottest rock and roll label in the business.

In 1973 Davis was forced out of Columbia over a dispute concerning misappropriation of expense account funds. He immediately regrouped by starting Arista Records which he named after the honor society he had belonged to in middle school. His transformed a one-time advertising jingle writer named Barry Manilow, with one inconsequential album on his resume, into a record-selling machine and Arista became a power player in the business. By the end of the 1970s Davis had built a reputation for jumpstarting the careers of one-time star acts, including the Kinks, Carly Simon and Dionne Warwick. Davis was beloved by artists for the intense personal relationships he forged with his artists.

That was what Aretha Franklin was seeking as she severed her ties to Atlantic Records. "I'm certain she noted what happen with Dionne (whose 1979 album Dionne had been the biggest seller of her career)," Davis recounted when discussing his recruitment efforts of Aretha after her Atlantic contract had lapsed. "We said that we would work as a partnership. That's what she had missed since the Jerry Wexler days."

Davis had a plan for bringing Aretha out of the 1960s and to the attention of 1980s audiences. First, he suggested songs that would span the musical spectrum highlighting Aretha's voice on everything from Vegas-style torch songs to soulful ballads to rollicking rhythm and blues. Then he surrounded her with successful producers and familiar session players from her early Atlantic hit albums like drummer Pretty Purdie and Motown bassist extraordinaire James Jamerson.

Davis also borrowed a page from Wexler's playbook to expose Aretha to as diverse an audience as possible. On November 17, 1980 Aretha was part of a Royal Variety Performance in the presence of Her Majesty Queen Elizabeth in London's Palladium Theatre. Also on the eclectic bill were such performers as Peggy Lee, Sammy Davis, Jr., Danny Kaye, Henry Mancini and Sheena Easton.

Aretha also took a star turn in John Belushi and Dan Aykroyd's *Blues Brothers* in 1980 as the wife of Matt "Guitar" Murphy and the owner of a soul food diner. She gets to lead a rousing rendition of her song "Think" that sets the Soul Food Cafe to rollicking. Prior to the Blues Brothers Aretha had only been called to Hollywood one time previously, for a small part in the ABC high school television series Room 222 in 1972.

Her first effort for Arista Records was called simply Aretha, in the manner of Dionne Warwick's revelatory self-titled Arista smash. The album did not climb to dizzying heights on the Billboard charts but the purpose of the nine tracks was primarily to re-establish Aretha as a phenomenal singer, rebuilding her credibility in the marketplace after years of presenting her lightly-promoted Atlantic music.

Aretha's sophomore outing for Arista, Love All The Hurt Way, garnered strong reviews and a cover of the Sam and Dave chestnut "Hold On! I'm Coming" produced her 11th Grammy Award - and first in seven years - for "Best Female R&B Vocal Performance." But overall sales for the album, while greater than Aretha, were still tepid. Undaunted, Davis recruited Luther Vandross to produce his next Aretha record.

Luther Vandross was born in 1951 into a musical family; his father was a crooner and his mother sang gospel. At the age of three he taught himself to play piano by ear, as Aretha had done when she was a child. Luther's sister Pat was a member of the vocal group The Crests in her teens; in a later configuration the group would have a chart-busting hit in "16 Candles." When he was a teenager in the 1960s his sisters took Luther to see Dionne Warwick, Diana Ross and Aretha. He developed an affinity for female singers and would one day found the first ever Patti LaBelle fan club.

After a brief stay at Western Michigan University, Vandross threw himself into music, writing songs and lending his three-octave tenor to back-up vocals for one-time idols Diana Ross and Barbra Streisand and many of their 1970s disciples like Roberta Flack, Bette Midler and Chaka Khan. He made his solo debut in 1981 on Never Too Much, writing and producing most of the material for what became one of the seminal rhythm and blues records of the decade. When Davis approached him to run the board for Aretha Franklin's next record he jumped at the opportunity, declaring himself an unabashed "Arethacologist."

Vandross brought a singer's sensibilities to the project and Aretha responded immediately. Vandross also provided a number of songs for the album, including the title track, "Jump to It," that became Aretha's first number one record in seven years. The album spent seven weeks atop the rhythm and blues charts in 1982 and became Aretha's first gold record since Sparkle. The 40-year old Aretha Franklin had officially made a hit "comeback" album. But the good vibrations were not to last.

Davis immediately reassembled his new chart-busting team for a follow-up record, but by the time Aretha went into the studios in 1983 there was a growing friction between Franklin and Vandross. Luther's career was in full ascendancy, and Aretha believed he was taking far too much credit for her own career revival and he needed to be reminded that there was a brilliant career already in place that he not only had nothing to do with but that had influenced his own development. Studio sessions deteriorated into shouting contests that Davis had to step in to referee while he pushed Get It Right to a bristly completion.

Rolling Stone wasted no time in dissecting the corpse of the finished product in its review: "Aretha Franklin teamed up with singer-song-writer-producer Luther Vandross last year to produce Jump to It, which featured a superbly consistent set of tunes and easily the finest singing Lady Soul has done in ten years. The second time around, this terrific twosome didn't quite get it right. Vandross' songs on Get It Right lack luster, perhaps because he's overextended himself: he's written material for his own album and for projects with Cheryl Lynn, Dionne Warwick, Diana Ross and Marcus Miller. And Aretha herself seems to be coasting this time out, unable or unwilling to transcend mediocre material as she has done so many times in the past."

Get It Right did not please the participants either. Aretha went so far as to file suit against Arista claiming that she had never been consulted on the hiring of Vandross as a producer. The suit quickly evaporated but the problems that had cropped up in her personal life around the same time did not so easily dissipate. Her marriage to Glynn Turman was crumbling and would end in divorce after six years in 1984. She moved back to Detroit to be closer to her comatose father in the last years of his life.

Aretha had always been wary of heights and often had to force herself onto airplanes to make her concert tours, but in the early 1980s her acrophobia became debilitating. After a near calamitous flight on a two-engine puddle jumper she could not fly at all. In 1984 she committed to play the title role on Broadway in a tribute to Mahalia Jackson called Sing, Mahalia, Sing! She rehearsed the numbers tirelessly in Detroit but when the time came to fly to New York for rehearsals she could not get on the plane. She has not flown since. When she balked at the ten-hour bus trip as well she was ordered to pay $250,000 to the producers for breach of contract.

Jump To It was still fresh in fans' minds and Aretha Franklin was already in need of another "comeback." The man she turned to in hopes of making it happen was Narada Michael Walden. Whereas Luther Vandross was bursting into a star when he was teamed with Aretha, Walden, a native of Kalamazoo, Michigan, had enjoyed a more modest career as a songwriter, performer and then a producer. While Vandross exuded confidence in his rhythm and blues arrangements, Walden had dabbled in jazz and funk and soul.

The collaboration began with a phone call and during the feel-each-other-out conversation Aretha described the process of meeting someone attractive and the cat-and-mouse game that sometimes ensued. "It's like 'who's zooming' who'," she called it, using an old euphemism from the urban streets. Right there Walden knew he had the title of the upcoming album.

When Who's Zoomin' Who was released in July 1985 critics acclaimed the album as containing Franklin's best work since the early days with Jerry Wexler in the 1960s. Through a variety of styles that included soul, Caribbean and gospel Walden let Aretha's voice dominate the record. For the first time since 1972 an Aretha album produced two Top Ten singles: the title track and "Freeway of Love" with E Street Band saxophonist Clarence Clemons playing saxophone.

Aretha told reporters that Who's Zoomin' Who was one of the best albums she had ever cut. Rolling Stone would eventually rank it among its 100 Greatest Albums on the '80s. It became the biggest selling studio album of Aretha's career and was certified platinum in both the United States and Canada. More importantly, Who's Zoomin' Who provided the gateway for Aretha to connect with the new MTV audiences that had eluded her since the cable television network debuted on August 1, 1981.

The mid-1980s were a time when superstar acts were using the music video network to send albums into the sales stratosphere - Michael Jackson (Thriller), Bruce Springsteen (Dancing in the Dark), Madonna (Like A Virgin) and Prince (Purple Rain) among them. Who's Zoomin' Who did the same promotional heavy lifting for Aretha Franklin. The video for "Freeway of Love" was filmed in Detroit and was put in heavy rotation on MTV where it became one of the most requested videos of the year.

Aretha, approaching her mid-forties, would not scale the commercial heights of Who's Zoomin Who again but her position as the Queen of Soul was now secure. In 1986 the Michigan Legislature passed a declaration recognizing Aretha's voice as a precious natural resource. The next year a duet with George Michael called "I Knew You Were Waiting (for Me)" produced the first Number One pop single of her career - twenty years after "Respect."

Also in 1987, Aretha Franklin became the first woman to be inducted into the Rock and Roll Hall of Fame. An artist is not eligible for inclusion in the Rock and Roll Hall of Fame until 25 years after the release of a debut album. In the 25 years since Aretha, her first album on Columbia, there had only been one year when Aretha Franklin did not release an album of original material - a record of unparalleled consistency. The one year that saw no new Aretha Franklin material was 1984, the year of her second divorce and her father's death.

In 1987, Aretha recorded a live gospel album over three nights in her father's New Bethel Baptist Church. Joining her on stage were her sisters Erma and Carolyn and gospel singer Mavis Staples. The power of the services was sabotaged by poor recording equipment and the record failed to resonate with the public as her now classic Amazing Grace from 1971 had done. Still, One Lord, One Faith, One Baptism captured the Gospel Music Association's Dove award for the best traditional gospel album of 1987.

After One Lord, One Faith, One Baptism Aretha no longer felt compelled to work every year to put out a new record. Between the gospel album's release and the end of the 20th century there would only be three new Aretha Franklin records. Through the Storm (1989) and What You See is What You Sweat (1991) left no one clamoring for the next Aretha record.

The easing of her recording schedule gave Aretha time to deal with personal issues that were washing over her during this period. Her sister Carolyn died of breast cancer in 1988 and two years later her brother Cecil succumbed to cancer as well. Her grandmother Rachel passed away in 1990. Erma would also die of cancer in 2002 and her half-brother Vaughn died two months after that. When that happened Aretha, then sixty years old, was the last remaining member of the Franklin family that had started humbly in Memphis so many years before.

With regards to her own health Aretha herself seemed never far from calamity. Her weight was a constant issue. She lost most of her excess pounds in the early 1990s only to finally give up smoking, breaking a two-pack-a-day habit, and gaining it all back in 1992. "After a concert you have expended a lot of energy and a piece of fruit or a glass of juice is simply not going to work when you would prefer a Quarter Pounder or a couple of tacos or the like," she confessed to fans worried about her weight. "But I declare I am going to win the war."

The 1990s saw Franklin tackling a variety of new projects. In 1993, to usher in the first Democratic President in a dozen years, Franklin was called upon to again perform at the presidential inauguration. She sang the fatalistic and somewhat incongruous to the occasion "I Dreamed a Dream" from *Les Misérables* for incoming President William Jefferson Clinton. She set liberal tongues to wagging when she appeared in a full-length mink coat and made no apologies to the animal rights crowd for her fashion choice. Four years later, her invitation to the Clinton inauguration included a presidential directive to leave the fur at home.

In July of that year she was included in "The Recording Event of The Decade" as 78-year old Frank Sinatra teamed with singing stars from across the musical spectrum for Duets. Aretha joined with the Chairman of the Board on "What Now My Love," a French standard from 1961 that had been covered in English by such diverse acts as Elvis Presley, Ben E. King and Shirley Bassey. After nearly a half century of recording and more than 50 albums, *Duets* became Sinatra's first triple platinum record.

Aretha took the Duets concept and created a one-hour television special for Fox TV by inviting Elton John, Rod Stewart, Smokey Robinson, Bonnie Raitt and Gloria Estafan to perform with her in a benefit for the Gay Men's Health Crisis. Franklin took the bus from her home in Bloomfield Hills, Michigan to New York City for the four-hour session to produce footage for the special. The extra takes were welcome for the big-name invitees who had to overcome a sense of awe in performing toe-to-toe with the Queen of Soul.

In 1994 Aretha Franklin was presented with a Grammy Lifetime Achievement Award for "creative contributions of outstanding artistic significance to the field of recording." The first six recipients of the honorarium were Bing Crosby, Frank Sinatra, Duke Ellington, Ella Fitzgerald, Irving Berlin and Elvis Presley to give an indication of the company Aretha was running in.

Aretha Franklin was again placed in esteemed company when she was tabbed to receive a Kennedy Center Honor Award. The prestigious awards were started in 1977 "to help build more enthusiasm for the performing arts and bring the public's attention to the artist's true place in society." The five honorees each year are recognized for their contributions to American culture. Celebrated along with Aretha in 1994 were Kirk Douglas, Morton Gould, Harold Prince and Pete Seeger; at the time 52-year old Aretha Franklin was the youngest entertainer to ever receive the honor. At the gala reception, intended to mimic England's command performances for the British Monarchy, Patti LaBelle, Levi Stubbs, the Four Tops and the New Bethel Baptist Church Choir provided one of the most memorable performances for Washington D.C. royalty in tribute to Aretha.

Despite the parade of honors for "lifetime achievement" Aretha Franklin was not wrapping up a career. Clive Davis showed his enduring faith in his superstar singer by signing Aretha to a three-year contract with Arista for a reported $10 million. She celebrated by getting accepted to The Juilliard School to study classical music. America's pre-eminent bastion for musical instruction started in 1905 when there was no music academy in America to rival the European conservatories. Frank Damrosch, the head of music education for New York City's public schools, was convinced that aspiring American musicians need not tramp across the Atlantic Ocean for their training. He coaxed money from James Loeb and modestly planned for 100 students but he had greatly underestimated the demand for high-quality musical training. The School quickly outgrew its original home at Fifth Avenue and 12th Street, and, in 1910, moved to new quarters on Claremont Avenue. When Augustus D. Juilliard, a wealthy textile merchant died in 1919, his will contained the largest single bequest for the advancement of music up to that time. Aretha kept intending to make it to Lincoln Center on a regular basis but a decade later she was still talking about finishing her classical education.

Aretha finally made it back into the studio in 1997 after a six-year absence, the longest fallow spell of her career. Soul music had not been lolling about waiting for her return. An energetic hip hop-inspired brand of soul had spawned a new crop of female singers that included Toni Braxton, Mary J. Blige, Mariah Carey and Lauryn Hill. Aretha Franklin was eager to make her mark with this new brand of soul and aligned herself with Sean "Puffy" Combs, Jermaine Dupri and Hill to produce A Rose Is Still a Rose, her 36th studio album.

In advance of the album's release, Aretha made a scheduled appearance on the Grammy Awards in February of 1998 to re-illuminate her star among music fans. She wowed the crowd with a reworked version of "Respect." What was not scheduled, however, was an illness that befell famed opera singer Luciano Pavarotti who was slated to be feted with a Lifetime Achievement Award. Aretha volunteered to stand in for the Italian tenor and with a half hour of preparation went on stage and performed "Nessun Dorma," one of the opera world's best known arias. When she finished the denouement to Giacomo Puccini's Turandot, delivered in Pavoratti's musical key, the crowd rewarded her with a standing ovation.

The following month "A Rose Is Still a Rose" reached a public audience. The title track, produced by Hill, found Aretha delivering worldly advice to a younger, confused woman and Franklin's vocal acrobatics called up a much younger Aretha for fans. The song became a crossover hit and Aretha Franklin had her first gold record in a dozen years. Despite having already been given a Lifetime Award from the Grammys, her performance earned her another Grammy nomination for rhythm and blues vocal performance. Although she would not win, Aretha had also served notice that she had not been put out to the musical pasture either.

In the twenty years since the making of the *Blues Brothers*, the movie had become a touchstone film for its generation. Fans would pepper everyday conversation with lines from the movie. John Belushi's untimely death had scuttled plans for a sequel but Dan Aykroyd always harbored visions of somehow paying homage to his friend and co-star. In 1998 he set out to make a tribute film that would find his Elwood Blues character released from jail, and a loose story was then crafted around what was essentially a collage of concert scenes.

That meant a return to Mrs. Maxwell. The Maxwells no longer run the Soul Food Café on Maxwell Street but have moved on to operate a Mercedes automobile dealership. But when Elwood Blues arrives to hijack Matt "Guitar" Murphy for a road tour he finds the same irascible Mrs. Murphy. In Blues Brothers 2000, Aretha once again chews up the scenery on screen as she regales her husband with the updated version of "Respect," backed by The Ridgeway Sisters and The Blues Brothers Band.

In 1999, Aretha tackled her autobiography for Villard Books. For the project she teamed up with New York-born David Ritz as ghostwriter. After graduating with honors at the University of Texas in 1966 Ritz embarked on a peripatetic writing career that wound in and around popular music. He contributed articles to *Rolling Stone* and provided liner notes for over 100 albums. He also wrote the lyrics for Marvin Gaye's "Sexual Healing" that became one of the biggest selling hit singles of all time in 1982.

Ritz set out to write a biography of Ray Charles, but decided the book would work better in Charles' voice and proposed they team up for an "autobiography." After the success of Brother Ray, Ritz followed the same formula with Smokey Robinson, Etta James, B.B. King and Jerry Wexler. His autobiography work won Ritz four Ralph J. Gleason Book Awards, making him the only four-time winner of the top honor for contributions to musical journalism. Gleason had been a founding editor of Rolling Stone and his name still remains on the magazine's masthead.

Ritz had also worked previously with Aretha before sitting down to plot out her life story. In 1992 he had won a Grammy Award for "Best Album Notes" for Queen of Soul: The Atlantic Recordings, an 86-track retrospective issued by Rhino Records. The Franklin autobiography *Aretha: From These Roots* did not break any revelatory ground when it was published. No light was shed about her teenage motherhood and one lover is referred to only as "Mr. Mystique." The closest she comes to providing grist for the gossip magazines are details of her open feuds with fellow singers such as Cissy Houston, mother of Whitney Houston who would become a Clive Davis darling at the same time Aretha was with Arista Records, and Gladys Knight. The *New York Times* called *Aretha: From These Roots* "a self-congratulatory yet entertaining autobiography."

One of Aretha's last music-related acts of the 20th century came when she was contacted by the White House Millennium Council, chaired by First Lady Hillary Clinton, to select a recording to be placed in a time capsule designed to be opened in 2100. Alongside a photo of Rosa Parks, a hunk of the Berlin Wall, and film footage of Neil Armstrong walking on the moon sits a copy of "Respect", in the unlikely event the music will be ignored by future generations.

In what was becoming an ingrained pattern of her later career five years passed after Franklin returned to the studio after "A Rose Is Still a Rose". "So Damn Happy" in 2003 sold well although it did not reach gold record status and produced another Grammy Award for "Best Traditional R&B Vocal Performance" on "Wonderful," a track written by Aleese Simmons, and Ron "Amen-Ra" Lawrence. In 2003 the National Academy of Recording Arts and Sciences had carved out a new category for "traditional" performances and Aretha snapped up another win in 2006 for a classic Burt Bacharach and Hal David tune, "A House Is Not a Home" that appeared on a tribute album to Luther Vandross, her old Arista sparring partner, who had died in 2005 following two decking years after a stroke.

In 2004 Aretha decided to end her relationship with Arista Records after 24 years and start her own label after she and Clive Davis could not come to agreement over a future direction for the 62-year old soul singer's career. She still owed Arista one more album and in 2007 she recorded duets with Fantasia Barrino and John Legend which were packaged with 14 other duets that Davis had collected during her time with the label. "Jewels in the Crown: All-Star Duets with the Queen" limped out onto the charts and "Put You Up on Game," the duet recorded with Fantasia, was the only single released. It became the final single of 65-year old Aretha's career and peaked at number 41 on the Hot R&B/Hip-Hop Songs.

Chapter 5: Later Years

Aretha had not employed a manager since her brother Cecil died in 1989, and immersing herself in the business end of music making did not thrill her. As a result, Aretha Records sputtered into existence - not that she was overly concerned about the idea of not being signed to a major record label at this point in her career.

In 2005 she took time out to accept the Presidential Medal of Freedom from George W. Bush. Harry S. Truman established the award in 1945, shortly after he came into office, to recognize "individuals who have made an especially meritorious contribution to the security or national interests of the United States, world peace, cultural or other significant public or private endeavors." It remains today the highest civilian award America can bestow.

That same year she became the second woman inducted into the United Kingdom Music Hall of Fame; Madonna had been the first. Another Hall of Fame where you will find Aretha Franklin is the Apollo Theater Legends Hall of Fame where the one-time Harlem burlesque house that opened in 1914 honors performers who have graced its stage. When the night club came under African-American ownership in 1934 after being a whites-only club a 17-year old Ella Fitzgerald and a 19-year old Billie Holiday made their debuts at the 125th Street Apollo Theater. Aretha performed for a series of sold-out shows at the Apollo in 1971, not long after the winners of an Amateur Night were The Jackson Five with a ten-year old Michael Jackson.

In 2007 the United Negro College Fund honored Aretha Franklin with its prestigious Award of Excellence for her decades-long support of education and the black community. She became the first female honoree to receive the award which had been celebrated with a three-hour concert tribute since 1980 known as "An Evening of Stars." Aretha had appeared on stage many times for the fundraiser, helping raise more than $200 million for access to higher education for the underprivileged.

In 2008 Franklin was tabbed by the National Association for the Advancement of Colored People (NAACP) to be feted at their 39th annual Image Awards Ceremony. She received the organization's Vanguard Award that "is presented to a person whose groundbreaking work increases our understanding and awareness of racial and social issues." Prior to Aretha Franklin the award had only been doled out to three recipients: movie directors Stanley Kubrick and Steven Spielberg, and Prince.

Franklin's ongoing philanthropy was recognized again in 2008 when she was presented with the annual MusiCares Person of the Year award from the National Academy of Recording Arts and Sciences. Established in 1991, the organization's MusiCares program brings needed health and medical assistance to financially struggling musicians. An all-star concert to raise funds takes place in advance of the Grammy Awards each year.

There were reports in the music press that Aretha was starting on a record for her new label at the age when most Americans were going in to retirement. But a heavy concert schedule stole time from the recording studio as did side projects like a duet with Mary J. Blige on a song for the movie *Bobby* that told the story of the 1968 assassination of leading Democratic Presidential candidate Robert F. Kennedy. Blige and Franklin shared a "Best Gospel Performance Vocal" Grammy for their efforts on "Never Gonna Break My Faith" from the Emilio Estevez film.

For the 2008 holiday season, Aretha teamed up with Borders Books to release a Christmas album exclusively in its stores. Franklin's first ever Christmas compilation was released by Los Angeles-based DMI Records. The fifty-one minutes of music contain only Yuletide standards and the Queen of Soul delivers them in a tame, traditional style. Aretha plays piano on several tracks and sons Eddie and Teddy chip in with vocals and guitar playing on the record. DMI released the record on its own in 2009 but "This Christmas" found a place only in the record collections of Aretha's most rabid fans.

In 2008, the American electorate returned a Democrat to the White House and once again Aretha Franklin was invited to perform at the inauguration. On January 20, 2009 Aretha serenaded Barack and Michelle Obama and an estimated 1.8 million people on the National Mall with a gospel-flavored version of "My Country 'Tis of Thee" at the West Front of the United States Capitol. As she did at the Clinton inauguration in 1992 Aretha made as much an impression with her fashion choices as she did with her stirring vocals.

Franklin wanted to wear a fur hat to keep her head warm in the anticipated January chill. For twenty years Aretha had her hats crafted by the Song family, South Korean immigrants who ran a hat-making business in Detroit. Luke Song discouraged the idea of fur since it would refract the light and likely cast her face in shadows. Aretha agreed and settled for a head-hugging gray cloche felt hat but also wanted it combined with a massive bow on top like another Song design in the shop. She also directed that the rhinestones in the hat be pared down to just an outline.

On an historic day when the country was inaugurating its first African-American President Aretha's hat rivaled Barack Obama for Internet buzz. The hat soon had its own Facebook page. Instead of going home to Detroit with Aretha it went to the Smithsonian Institution. The Rock and Roll Hall of Fame borrowed "The Hat" to go on a memorabilia exhibition tour. After Barack Obama leaves office "The Hat" is slated to go on permanent display at the Obama presidential library.

After Barack Obama was re-elected in 2012 Aretha was not invited to perform at the inauguration, marking the first Democratic Presidential inauguration which would not feature an appearance by the Queen of Soul in 36 years. The press, however, was still talking about "The Hat" from 2009. When Katy Perry made her appearance at the ceremony she paid tribute to Aretha by sporting a miniature version of the celebrated headgear.

In 2010 Franklin began experiencing pain in her side and was forced to cancel a performing tour. She underwent surgery but never revealed the nature of her illness which led to rampant speculation that she was battling pancreatic cancer. She returned from the hospital declaring that the mystery surgery on December 2, 2010 had "been a complete success" and reports of her having cancer were erroneous.

A star-studded "get well card" was planned for the upcoming Grammy Awards in February with Yolanda Adams, Christina Aguilera, Jennifer Hudson, Martina McBride and Florence Welch leading the tribute. Within a few months the Queen of Soul had shed 85 pounds and the surgical procedure was reported to have been a lap band and breast reduction. Despite the unlikelihood of losing that amount of weight in such a s short period of time with good eating habits, Franklin denied those reports as well. With no public clarification, all that can be definitively said of that time in Aretha Franklin's life is that she was forced to cancel concerts, went to the hospital, received successful surgery, returned to the public eye in good health, and lost 85 pounds along the way.

In 2011, the long-awaited studio album from Aretha Records was released. Aimed at a maturing audience "Aretha: A Woman Falling Out of Love" received an icy welcome from critics. Once again she leaned on duets, including one with her son Eddie. It was their first appearance on record together. Aretha's son Teddy often appeared live with his mother, backing her up on guitar. The record only moseyed to number 54 on the Billboard charts and did little more than provide a marker for Aretha's 50th year in show business.

By the arrival of her 70th birthday in 2012 the list of awards and laurels for Aretha Franklin was long and impressive. One, however, seemed overdue. While she was the first woman inducted into Rock and Roll Hall of Fame twenty-five years earlier Aretha did not get the call into the Gospel Music Hall of Fame until 2012. The Gospel Music Association had begun their Hall of Fame back in 1971 to recognize meaningful contributions in all forms of gospel music. Even though Aretha turned her back on gospel music as a teenager she had more than established her gospel bonafides in the years since. She won three Grammys for gospel performances and Amazing Grace was still the best-selling live gospel album of all time forty years after its release.

One area of Aretha Franklin's life where she certainly did not qualify for any Hall of Fame was in romantic relationships. Shortly after 2012 began Aretha made news with the announcement that she was engaged to be married for the third time and that the ceremony would take place on a yacht in Miami Beach that summer. The groom was William "Willie" Wilkerson who was certainly not an unknown name to long-time Aretha fans.

Franklin and Wilkerson first met in the 1980s when he was a firefighter standing in line to get Aretha's autograph in Detroit. He asked her to sign the cast on his leg and a few years later *Jet* magazine was trumpeting in its headlines that "Aretha Franklin Finds Happiness With New Love In Her Life." She even snuck him into her music video for "Jimmy Lee." For years Franklin referred to Wilkerson in the press as her "forever friend" and they were often photographed together at basketball games and public appearances with his role in her life described as "escort."

The announcement caught Aretha watchers by surprise, but even before the rumor mill had a chance to grind the engagement was scuttled after only three weeks. "Will and I have decided we were moving a little too fast, and there were a number of things that had not been thought through thoroughly," Franklin explained. "There will be no wedding at this time."

As she headed into her seventies Franklin continued to fill her trophy case with awards and honoraria. She received honorary doctorates from Harvard University, Yale University, Case Western University, the University of Pennsylvania, Berklee College of Music and others. Dr. Franklin was still, however, not ready to retire her famous vocal chords.

At her 70th birthday party she announced plans for her 39th studio album. Once again Clive Davis would be helming the project. "Although we took a little recording break, our strong friendship always continued," the legendary hit maker explained. "I had this concept of having the Queen of Soul interpret diva classics by Dinah Washington, Etta James, Gladys Knight, Gloria Gaynor, Barbra Streisand, Diana Ross, Whitney Houston, Alicia Keys, Adele among others."

With the album due for a late 2014 release Davis took pains to assure the industry that this would not be a just-for-old-times farewell outing. "Aretha's new album is purely and simply sensational. She's on fire and vocally in absolutely peak form. What a thrill to see this peerless artist still showing the way, still sending shivers up your spine, still demonstrating that all contemporary music needs right now is the voice. What a voice," he declared. And so, once again, Aretha Franklin's fans are doing what they have been doing for six decades: waiting to hear from the Queen of Soul.

Chapter 6: Legacy

A look at baseball's record book reveals staggering records that will never be approached: Cy Young's 511 lifetime pitching wins, Tris Speaker's 792 career doubles, Ty Cobb's .367 career batting average. To a major league baseball player in the 21st century those accomplishments are inconceivable. Aspiring singers must be similarly amazed when they look at the numbers put up by Aretha Franklin in her career: 39 studio albums, 20 number-one R&B singles, 44 Grammy nominations and 18 wins.

Aretha Louise Franklin was not a groundbreaker. She just did what she does better and longer than anyone else. She recorded her first major label album when Dwight D. Eisenhower was in the White House and then sang at the inauguration of Barack Obama. She performed on American Bandstand in 1962 and American Idol in 2013.

She was able to remain a force in the recording industry all that time despite a tumultuous personal life. While she was fortunate to team professionally with men like John Hammond, Jerry Wexler and Clive Davis, her domestic partners seldom provided support during her career, and at times worked actively to bring it harm, forcing her to become intensely private about her rarely discussed life away from music.

It was the music that drove her always, pushing her past obstacles that would have road-blocked lesser wills than Franklin's. She has not been on an airplane in more than 30 years after a nerve-shaking flight, yet she has kept up a concert presence across the United States that has cemented her reputation as the Queen of Soul. She did not know how to read music and yet taught herself to play piano, becoming so skilled that Keith Richards would be wowed when he recorded with her. "A lot of people forget that on top of an incredible voice, she's an incredible piano player," gushed the Rolling Stones guitarist. "She comes up with amazing musical ideas. You never have to worry about the tempo because she just sets it."

But always with Aretha Franklin associations return to her voice, that four-octave instrument that emerged from her father's church in Detroit when she was a teenager. When *Rolling Stone* magazine gathered a panel of 179 experts in 2008 to rank the greatest singers of the rock and roll era: Ray Charles, James Brown, Sam Cooke and Elvis Presley were all jostling to be recognized as the best-ever vocalist but in the end, they were all forced to step aside. The experts agreed that the Greatest Singer of All Time has been Aretha Franklin.

Bibliography

Bates, Karen Grigsby, National Public Radio, "Aretha Franklin Was Already Famous, But Her Hat-Maker Wasn't," January 21, 2013.

Bego, Mark, Aretha Franklin: The Queen of Soul, New York: St. Martin's Press, 1989.

Davis, Clive, The Soundtrack of My Life, New York: Simon & Schuster, 2013.

Dobkin, Matt, I Never Loved a Man the Way I Love You: Aretha Franklin, Respect, and the Making of a Soul Music Masterpiece, St. Martin's Press, 2004.

Eagle, Bob L. and LeBlanc, Eric S., Blues: A Regional Experience, Santa Barbara, CA: Prager, 2013.

Ebony, "The New Aretha," October 1974.

Ebony, "The Swingin' Aretha," March 1964.

Graff, Gary, Detroit Free Press, "Queen Of Soul Reigns Supreme On Fox TV's Special, 'Duets'," May 7, 1993.

Hammond, John and Townsend, Irving, John Hammond on record, New York: Penguin Records, 1981.

Hau, Louis, Reuters, Aretha Franklin does "own thing" with new album, March 19, 2010.

McAvoy, Jim, Aretha Franklin, New York: Chelsea House Publishers, 2002.

McKinley, James C., Jr., *The New York Times*, "Franklin Plans Album With Clive Davis," March 27, 2012.

Nesmith, Tammy Sill, *The New York Times*, "Aretha," October 31, 1999.

Pareles, Jon, *The New York Times*, "The Queen of Soul Takes Control," November 4, 2007.

Salvatore, Nick, Singing in a Strange Land: C. L. Franklin, the Black Church, and the Transformation of America, New York: Little, Brown and Company, 2005.

Stutz, Colin, Billboard, "Clive Davis Says Aretha Franklin Is 'On Fire' on New Album of Diva Classics," September 18, 2004.

Waldron, Clarence, *Jet*, "Aretha: Life On The Road Forces The Queen Of Soul To Find A New Strategy In Her Battle With Weight," November 19, 2007.

Ward, Ed, National Public Radio, "Aretha Franklin Before Atlantic: The Columbia Years," February 27, 2013.

Werner, Craig, Higher Ground: Stevie Wonder, Aretha Franklin, Curtis Mayfield, and the Rise and Fall of American Soul, New York: Crown Publishing, 2004.

CPSIA information can be obtained
at www.ICGtesting.com
Printed in the USA
FSHW01n0642200818
51579FS

9 781502 500007